The BONDAGE of GIVING

Has the Church taught it wrong?

William Vines, Jr., D.Min.
Marian Brannon Jones, D.Th.

ISBN-13:978-1721980215
ISBN-10:1721980210

You and I must be perfectly willing to part with anything at any moment. It matters not whether I leave two thousand dollars or merely two. What matters is whether I can leave whatever I have without a twinge of regret.

- Watchman Nee

Contents

Foreword

Making our way out of the stockyards' administration office, I fixed my gaze. Staring with deep intent, I read left-to-right, over and over again. It was real. Making it official, the letters of my name were impressed on the blue-green paper by archaic, Times-New Roman, size 12 font. A check made payable to me. My cow, Taffy, through her offspring, had made me rich!

Check in hand, my feet clogged and my body danced.

Two years earlier, my dad had given me my first heifer. At the moment of reception (fresh from the taste of a Smoky Mountain specialty gift sent to our family table by my Aunt Sue), I deemed Taffy an appropriate name for the matriarch of my herd. And, on this day, my cow couldn't have been any more sugary-sweet!

I was going to buy a new Spalding basketball, three games for my SEGA, a new pair of Air Jordan's, and something else — I just hadn't thought of it yet. I could hardly wait to cash my check!

Now in the front passenger seat of my father's single-cab Ford F-150 4x4, the mud-grip tires rotating on the pavement provided a humming soundtrack for my daydreams of becoming America's next cattle baron, which, I might add, were the direct result of my enthrallment with the reading and re-reading of my name at the center of a business-size check.

Deep within the lands of fantasy, I was just about to buy my first farm when the firm voice of my often silent father gently invaded my entrepreneurial vision. He informed me that upon arrival at the bank, we would be opening a checking account. This new addition to my non-existent financial portfolio would give me the opportunity, as a pre-teen businessman, to write checks - checks to purchase all of the things on my wish list! But when he notified me that this would not be the primary reason for opening the bank account, I was stunned. Like a curious puppy, I turned my head to face him. It was then that my father's words penetrated my over-sided, red, Ralph D. Roy Real Estate cap, found their way to my developing mind, and laid a cornerstone in my initially bewildered heart.

Little did I know, the truth he shared on a three-mile drive from Russell County Stockyards to First National Bank would come to be a principle of living that, twenty-five years later, still sits foundationally at the core of my approach to all things financial, "In this house, God comes first."

On the other side of his statement, he quoted Malachi 3:8-10 and shared his personal experience with the fulfillment of God's faith-activated promise. He let me know that if I wanted to experience the same - and more – then, the firstfruits of my life should be given to God. It was only then that I realized an opportunity to embrace this truth would be the primary reason for our trip to the bank on that morning.

I wasn't certain how to best process the fact that it would be my second check which was going to be written for the new leather, indoor/outdoor basketball instead of the first one. After our venture into the bank's new accounts office, I vividly remember the light-blue checks arriving in the mail a few days later. I was proud to see the University of Kentucky Wildcats logo (for which I had paid extra) in the upper left-hand corner!

Opening the box and laying the first book of checks out on the table, I borrowed, from my father's left-front shirt pocket, his favorite pen. And, following his guidance, I wrote my first check.

In my best handwriting, I endorsed the sum of twenty-five dollars (1/10 of the gross income from the sale of my bull) to be made payable to Freedom Church of God. In that moment, it was just the name of my childhood church and an investment that I was delusional to believe was delaying my development as a cattle farmer & NBA prospect. But I now consider the words on that first check to be prophetic, especially the first one: "Freedom." All of these years later, my soul stirs with thankfulness as I contemplate the first check I ever wrote was sown into FREEDOM.

In the pages to follow, my good friend, Dr. Bill Vines, and his accomplished co-author, Dr. Marian Jones, unveil the Biblical principles behind why my father's stockyard conversation with his 12-year-old son has resulted in the manifestation of a generational blessing that has broken the bondage of a poverty mentality from our family and resulted in financial freedom that is exceedingly, abundantly, above all we could have ever asked for or imagined.

We were once a family, during my father's childhood, who lived in a decrepit farmhouse with no indoor plumbing. It was sure to have been condemned in any city due to structural instability. But years later, due to God's faith-activated blessings, our once visibly impoverished lineage now collectively overflows with blessing, with ownership of hundreds of acres of highly sought-after farmland, multiple rental properties, an ever-expanding consulting business, and with more blessings which continue to flow every day. The breakthrough has little to do with us — no one in our family has a substantial educational degree and no prior entrepreneurial experience. However, the triumph has everything to do with God and His willingness to honor His promises.

Astounded by the continued goodness of God, a few months ago, I found myself behind the steering wheel of my truck, its mud-grip tires providing the soundtrack for the daydreams of my 12-year old entrepreneurial daughter. We were driving from an Arts & Crafts Expo to First National Bank. She was making preparation to write her first check...

It's now your opportunity to begin a theological ride through Scriptures with Dr. Vines and Dr. Jones and enjoy the scenery of blessing at every overlook. It is with great expectation, I anticipate your arrival in the land of the free!

Yours for His glory,

Eric Gilbert

Part One

The Spirit of Giving

Introduction

"Give, give, give. That's all the church wants me to do. I thought this was supposed to be about loving and caring for one another, being a good and kind person, going to church – not all this giving stuff. Every time I go to a church service, or listen to ministers on TV, all they want is for me to give them my money."

This is an all-too-familiar attitude that many people have when it comes to the church. And chances are, you have heard it and maybe you've even had similar thoughts yourself. Back in the 1970's, televangelism was born and introduced mainstream watchers to the idea of "seed-faith" giving. The premise was, "give to this program, and God will bless your socks off." Equally as popular a message was, "God wants us all to be rich and the more you give (to my ministry), the richer you will be." (Honestly, if they really believed that, they would have sent all their viewers a check!)

We are paraphrasing and purposefully being a little cynical because that is the message people heard. The sad thing about this message, along with many messages on giving, is that it fails to paint a complete picture of how giving is intertwined in the loving, merciful, totality of who God is - His nature and character. A multitude of believers gave to the rich and famous evangelists and TV ministries "in the name of God." The prosperity message struck at the heart of humanism and prompted people to "give in order to get." We certainly aren't saying that everyone who gave was wrong to do so, but there was a whole lot of abuse and misuse of money that was supposed to have been given for Kingdom work that sure didn't look like God. Even today there are echoes of that era of misguided, self-centered prosperity - gain for personal glory.

There is a lot of deception concerning scripture, not just in the area of money and wealth, but in every area. It is our desire to give an accurate view of our great God while providing a biblical foundation for the three monetary ways Christians are taught to give (tithe, offering, and firstfruits) by illuminating Old Testament scriptures and how God's law transitions with Jesus. More than likely, if you are reading this, you already have a pretty good foundation for the tithe and offering - at least, that's what we've found. We've also found that there is really very little teaching or understanding about firstfruits, and for that reason, it will be the greater focus of the three when we look at them biblically.

As in all "Christian living" teaching topics, giving has, for the most part, been reduced to an action, a "do this" guideline that will please the Lord. You know those guidelines, the ones we refer to when we want to feel good about ourselves. "Well, I don't do this, and I do that, and I don't do that thing you're not supposed to do, so I'm okay with God." Again, "actions" that we think will keep us in God's good graces. So, though we feel there is a great need to explain giving - and specifically firstfruits giving - we can't do so without stressing that giving, as well as everything we "do," should be an outflow of a heart that is molded by the consistent flow of His presence. Giving should be because He moves in us to do so, not because "He said so."

When John the Baptist was in prison and about to be beheaded, he sent word to Jesus. His question, "Are you the Messiah or do we look for another?" Jesus responded with, "Tell John what you have seen and heard . . . the blind receive their sight, and the lame walk, the lepers are cleansed, and the deaf hear, the dead are raised up, and the poor have the gospel preached to them." Jesus did not answer John with a discourse of sayings, but actions. The words of Jesus had weight because they were truth, but without the miraculous actions, He would have been merely a wise man. It was what Jesus *did* that He said we could do

> *Giving should be because God moves in us to do so, not because He said so.*

when He went to the Father. And what Jesus did was to give His all freely and willingly because it was His nature and the nature of the Father. His giving was the end point of that which was in His heart to do. (Action released from Spirit!) He had already given His life before He died on the cross. The Sanhedrin had already crucified Jesus before the cross too. Their heart was set on it from the beginning of Jesus' earthly ministry.

Regardless of actions or outcomes, there is a beginning point to everything. It starts with a thought, a feeling, an impression or response. As Christians, we should want that beginning point to ALWAYS be God. Without Him, without the finished work of Christ, and without the Holy Spirit's leading, there is nothing humanity can offer which would be worthy of giving or accomplishing which would have any eternal value. Oh, if we could only grasp that! The Apostle Paul stated in Galatians 2:20, "*I am crucified with Christ: nevertheless I live; yet not I, **but Christ lives in me:** and the life which I now live in the flesh I live by the faith of the Son of God, who loved me, and gave himself for me.*"

How is it possible for us to live in the flesh without the flesh? It is only possible because we live in the Spirit. Our flesh continues to abide in this world, but it is our Spirit, the Spirit of God *in* us, which allows life to continue. Our flesh is already dead but we are tethered to God through His Spirit, and Spirit never dies. And it is HIS Spirit in us which is to be the beginning point of our every *Godly* action. The first condition in GODLY giving, therefore, is God's presence. Sure, we can give, but if it isn't giving that's released by His grace, it will not carry His divine seed of blessed hope and holiness. We should all be permeated with the knowledge that *"It is not I who gives but Christ who gives through me."* Is that the way you think of it when you give?

Having that mindset and internal motivation ensures that everything we do, everything we GIVE, indeed our every action, is merely us participating in the transference of what is His. We are not in bondage to it. It is not something we *have* to do. It is not our response to a command. It is not something for which we will necessarily miss heaven if we don't do, but it is something that *we get to do*! What a privileged people we are! We, of such lowly estate, get to participate in the conveyance of Almighty God's great plan for His Kingdom!

~ 1 ~
In God We Trust?

Did you know that "In God We Trust" is the official motto of the United States? It isn't just a slogan on our currency, it was actually adopted as our motto, replacing the Latin phrase, *E pluribus unum* - "One out of many." You may find it comforting, as many do, to read "In God We Trust" on our money when so many people are fighting to have it removed. But the fact remains that, as a nation, we recognized the importance of trusting God - at least in word if not in deed. The history of our motto is thought-provoking and we challenge you to discover how that decision began. While certainly not the focus in this writing, the reasons and motivations for actions, like adopting this motto, show the significance of beginnings. Making "In God We Trust" the official motto began as a thought, an idea born, no doubt, in the spirit of a man, before it was released, nominated, selected, and designated. Before he spoke the words, the idea was born and released. The same can be said of God when forming this world in which we live. Creation was released in Him before He spoke the words, "Let there be."

Liken that to our giving. Before we truly give to God, we must truly release, and that is only accomplished when His Spirit moves in us and motivates us to do so. This must be a conscious, willing decision, *not a reluctant routine.*

If you've ever seen a video of a human egg being fertilized, you'll see how once the egg's surface is permeated, it instantly changes. Scientists have recently discovered that there is actually a zinc explosion, a literal "spark." As believers, we know this is the moment a soul from God's hand is delivered. This is the beginning of life. Around nine months later, the human is fully formed and manifested, but *life began with that spark, marking God's hand.* When our giving begins with the spark of God's spirit, it is released by Him and for Him, just as our very lives given by Him are for Him.

We are reminded of a well-to-do young man who was convinced that he should not give to a church because he had no say-so in how the money was spent! It was evident that he had not released his money by God's Spirit. Even if he had given money to that or any church, the giving would have emanated from his own volition and not a loving response to God. Would the church have benefited? Absolutely. But the blessing returned to that man would have been for his glory and not God's. The church, once the gift was received, had the opportunity and responsibility of consecrating it to the Lord, thus changing the blessing upon it. (Churches, as well as individuals, are held spiritually accountable for what they receive too!)

If we do not release from a heart that is sparked (motivated) and moved by His Spirit, it is not released *TO* Him or in His name and will not be attached to Him at all! That is what separates those of us in Christ, and our giving, from the world. There are many, many people in this world who give generously – people who don't even purport to be Christian. People give billions of dollars each year to help others and do good things for the world. Some of them are feeding the hungry, giving clothes to the poor, visiting those in prison.

What's the difference between what these people are doing and what we, through Christ, do? These people love humanity. Isn't that what we are to do? They strive to be good people and to bring peace. Isn't that what we are to do? So what's the difference? The Spirit of God is the difference. The Spirit of God motivates us BECAUSE of God. Can God move on the heart of the wicked to give? Oh, yes. He is a sovereign God. We have heard many stories of non-believers being prompted to give large amounts of money for Kingdom work. There are several billionaires in this country who give generously to social programs, but they cannot give their way to a heavenly eternity.

The revenue laws in this country make financial giving beneficial, and that's a good thing for both social welfare and even Kingdom programs. Large corporations give for financial gain and also glory, a bragging point to make them look good in the eyes of the public. Sadly, some believers give for the same reasons. Some church-goers actually tithe so they won't look bad in the eyes of their pastor. Some like to make donations so that their names will be forever engraved on benches and buildings. The Bible tells us they, indeed, already have their reward in doing those good things. But doing good things does not make us a better person, only God does that. We could give the world (or gain the world) and it would still be the world! When our giving is from a heart filled with His presence and moved by His leading, what we give is holy because it has been touched by the Father. If we give even one quarter of a penny (a widow's mite) from that 'release' point, it is far greater than a million dollars that are attached to the world or have that human release point. For those in the world, giving makes them better people in the eyes of the world. But for those in Christ, giving makes us better people because of Christ and in the eyes of God.

> *Doing good does not make us better, only God does that!*

Giving reveals to God that we trust Him. We trust Him so much that we give Him what the world sees as valuable, and the world values flesh, fame, and fortune! When we give God what is valuable to us, it makes *us* valuable to Him because we trust Him more than we trust the world.

What the world values, the world exalts. Just watch five minutes of television and you'll see what is exalted: fleshly pleasure, social status, and lavish lifestyles. What should be private is publically flaunted, what should be unashamed is shamed, dishonesty and violence is justified, scantily-clad shapely bodies are revered, and the wealthy stars and sports professionals are more celebrated than those who live righteously.

Flesh, fame, and fortune has always been valuable to the world. That's how Jesus was tempted. (Matthew 4:1-11)

> FLESH: *And when the tempter came to him, he said, If thou be the Son of God, command that these stones be made bread. But he answered and said, 'It is written, Man shall not live by bread alone, but by every word that proceeds out of the mouth of God.'*

> FAME: *Then the devil took him up into the holy city, and set him on a pinnacle of the temple, And said unto him, If thou be the Son of God, cast thyself down: for it*

is written, He shall give his angels charge concerning thee: and in their hands they shall bear thee up, lest at any time thou dash thy foot against a stone. Jesus said unto him, 'It is written again, Thou shalt not tempt the Lord thy God.'

FORTUNE: *Again, the devil taketh him up into an exceeding high mountain, and showeth him all the kingdoms of the world, and the glory of them; And saith unto him, All these things will I give thee, if thou wilt fall down and worship me. Then saith Jesus unto him, 'Get thee hence, Satan: for it is written, Thou shalt worship the Lord thy God, and him only shalt thou serve.'*

Jesus overcame because His trust was in God, not those worldly things.

Abraham trusted God and was willing to give his only son in obedience to God's request. That sounds kind of severe doesn't it? That sounds like an extreme sacrifice and, undeniably, it was. Why would God ask for such a huge sacrifice from Abraham? Because He had a huge blessing awaiting

Abraham. God knew what He wanted Abraham to do and to become. He was in a covenant relationship with Abraham, where He'd promised to make Abraham the father of many nations IF Abraham would walk perfectly before Him. That's a huge promise! But in order to do such a great thing *for* God, Abraham was called upon to give a great thing *to* God and the same is true for us today! We are in a covenant relationship with God. He knows the plans He has for us. What we are willing to give to Him will determine how those plans will unfold.

It is doubtful that Abraham could have seen what God would require of him when he first received God's promise. What if Abraham had not trusted God and refused to offer his son? We are convinced he would have lost him anyway and perhaps Abraham would have lost his own life without becoming the man God desired him to become or achieve all that God desired for him to achieve. Surely we would be reading Abraham's sad story of fear and doubt and the story of obedience of someone else God raised up to be the father of many nations. *Lord, may we all be willing to fulfill the story you have for us!*

Abraham's life, though a much longer span than lives today, was eventually over. His time on earth in this dimension came to an end. His true legacy was not one of financial wealth, but spiritual wealth. He is on the other side of eternity now as we all will be sooner than we realize.

But even on this side of eternity, our money, belongings, possessions – all that we have – can disappear or be destroyed at any time. So many times, when natural disasters occur, survivors who are interviewed will say, "We lost everything, but we lived." Things can be replaced but death is eternal. Things are temporary and the value we place on them will determine to what extent we will be distressed with their loss. If we place too much value on them, if we consider our accumulated 'things' as treasures, we will be shattered when they are gone. God desires our treasure and worth to be with those things that can never be destroyed or taken from us - **Himself, His Kingdom (the Church), and the people *He* has put in our lives**.

> *Lay not up for yourselves treasures upon earth, where moth and rust corrupts, and where thieves break through and steal: But lay up for yourselves treasures in heaven,*

> *where neither moth nor rust corrupts, and*
> *where thieves do not break through nor*
> *steal: For where your treasure is, there will*
> *your heart be also.* **Matthew 6:19-21**

This scripture is a clear spiritual truth and presents us with a challenge – not "Where is your treasure?" but "Where is your heart?" The two are inseparable and reveal to God whether or not He can trust us. Treasure is not about financial wealth, but where your **trust lay** and what you perceive as valuable. The ultimate trust of man by God is not with money, but with people. We are valuable to God and the way we treat one another and love one another is of utmost importance to Him. Can God trust you with people? Well here is the big question for all who are in Christ, "How can God TRUST you with the lives of people if He can't trust you with a dollar?" The fact is, overcoming the temptation to store up treasures on earth is a sure sign that God *can* trust you with His people and positions of leadership in His Kingdom. It is folly to think God will open the door

What we release and give TO God reveals our trust IN God.

to your divine destiny, or put you in a place of Christian leadership, while you are not trusting Him enough to lay all your possessions (possessions which HE gave you anyway) at His feet! Lord, help us to be ever-reminded of Abraham's story.

Trusting God changes our hearts so that we are becoming more like Him, learning to focus on what is **eternally important** - the spiritual things of God which *never fade away*, and not the **temporary** things of this world which will. God loves us and wants us to continue to grow spiritually, being transformed, becoming more and more in love with Him and attached to Him, and less and less like the world and attached to the world.

What we *release* to God and *give* to God reveals our trust in God. The more we give to His Kingdom of our finances, time, and abilities, the more room we make for God, and the more we allow Him to change us. And the more He changes us, the more we desire to give of our finances, time, and abilities. His nature, once imbedded in our hearts, will be the beginning point, a spark for our every action, making everything we do have the aura of His touch. Isn't that the epitome of giving glory to God?

A scripture about giving that we Christians love (and love to quote), comes from Luke 6:38:

> *Give, and it shall be given unto you, good measure, pressed down, and shaken together, and running over, shall men give into your bosom. For with the same measure that ye mete withal it shall be measured to you again.*

There's more to this scripture than the financial blessing received when one gives. The focus has usually been on monetary measurements, when what Jesus is showing us is not quantity, but quality. He is talking about the heart of the giver. When you release your giving, and it comes from a heart entrenched in God's love, giving because He moves in you and has moved on you to do so (and not because you are in bondage to it), it will send a spiritual signal - His *spark* of holiness - that will attract His moving in the hearts of others (the men that shall give unto you!). That's why what you receive is so much more than what you give. That's why we're told in the Bible, "It's more blessed to give than to receive." Everything God touches explodes with His goodness and is marked with His holiness.

It is His measure we want to use when giving because when we do, His measure is what will be used as others give to us. And His measurement is such *good* measure, that it is "pressed down, shaken together, and running over!" It isn't the width of the portal we open to receive, it's the depth!

If the Christian community really understood that this is the perpetual, exponential nature of God and allowed Him to rule their heart, we could change the world! If we would allow everything we receive to flow through us and be touched by God, when we give, it would be compounded by His blessing. Can you visualize that? If you receive $1 (even if it was not blessed when you received it) and you commit it to God and allow His Spirit to lead you in how you use it, when it is circulated back into the *world*, it will have His attached blessing with His intended purpose! Whatever comes to us, if allowed to go 'through' His Spirit in us, will be changed because of Him. Money is indeed the world's system, but when it goes through the hands of a Christian, it should be altered!

Don't become complacent where giving and receiving are concerned. We caution you against giving habitually or lawfully and implore you to give deliberately and conscientiously. Before you write that check, present that gift, serve, use your abilities, or make any offering, be sure to pause, recognize Who moves in you, Who prompts and motivates you, and release it with His purpose. Even when paying a bill, recognize that you have the ability to do so because God caused resources to come to you and 'release' it as a blessing from God. You may even consider this prayer:

> Father, I thank You for being my provision. As I release this _____ (FIB), I release it with Your blessing. Maybe I can't trace every penny, but You can. And I declare that since You are my Lord, and You reign in my heart, that whatever I touch, You touch, and whatever You touch has Your mark upon it. I declare the mark of Jesus on every offering I give, every ability I use, and every service that I render. And just as Your Word works to perform Your will, may that which You work through me work to perform Your perfect will. Let me be a conduit through which Your will is performed (and sent to perform) throughout the world. AMEN!

It goes back to approval. Do you want to be approved by man's standard or by God's standard? The wise choose God's standard of measurement. IN GOD WE TRUST!

God responds when His people
are kind and generous.

*Blessed are those who have regard for
the weak; the Lord delivers them in
times of trouble. The Lord protects
and preserves them. They are counted
among the blessed in the land, he does
not give them over to the desire of
their foes. The Lord sustains them on
their sickbed and restores them from
their bed of illness. Psalms 41:1-3
NIV*

~ 2 ~
# True Prosperity

The Bible teaches, "Faith is the substance of things hoped for, the evidence of things not seen." Faith is one of those high impact words in the Bible. They say that the ultimate fame for a person is when he or she is known internationally by one name (Elvis, Bono, Madonna, Sting, . . . JESUS!) Similarly, in the Christian community, faith is right up there with the stand-alone words like love, hope, mercy and grace. Faith means that the expected outcome will be made manifest and reveals that the conviction was not based on an imagination of the mind but the reality of the Christ-filled heart. Before we see it with our eyes, we believe it in our heart.

The Lord recently gave us another quote-worthy statement concerning faith: "Faith is trusting that God's plan for us, and His will for us, is what's best for us." That is the ultimate factor of our well-being – God's plan and will! And don't you agree that His plan and will is going to be different for each of us? Truly believing and accepting that means that we have absolutely placed everything, from position to provision, wholly in His care, with the knowledge that all we have, and all we have the ability to become, is because of Him. That being said, we should be willing to do with ourselves AND our possessions whatever He asks. But what if we are asked to have no possessions? What if we are asked to live meagerly? Just reading those two questions would make many people cringe and say, "God doesn't want me poor. He wants me to prosper!" There it is. That is the big error. The world sees prosperity as financial wealth because that's what the world values. But God doesn't value what the world values.

The prosperity message pretty much taught that if you were wealthy it was a sign of God's favor. If your church was blessed with growth, it was God's blessing. People became haughty with the Word of God, and left no room for the sovereignty of God.

Command those who are rich in this present world not to be haughty or to put their hope in wealth, which is so uncertain, but to put their hope in God, who richly provides us with everything for our enjoyment. Command them to do good, to be rich in good deeds, and to be generous and willing to share. In this way they will lay up treasure for themselves as a firm foundation for the coming age, so that they may take hold of the life that is truly life.
1 Timothy 6:17-19

Remember, Jesus said, "Foxes have dens and birds have nests, but the Son of Man has no place to lay his head." He was talking about the cost of following Him. It's not that God doesn't want us to prosper financially, but prosperity in itself means that everything we do and who we are, is good according to God's will and His plan for our lives. If we give just to gain financially, we have no concept of true prosperity. When John wrote to Gaius (3 John), "I wish above all things that you prosper and be in health, even as your soul prospers," his prayer was not for riches, but for the well-being of Gaius in his journey with the Lord. That kind of prosperity is spiritual!

Now before you get the idea that we are anti-wealth, we are not. But we are pro-*balanced life* and the way to a balanced Christian life is a balanced Word of God. We remember that before the "prosperity" teaching was popularized, Christians had to endure the "poverty" message, where suffering for Jesus was the norm and accumulating wealth was for the Judases. We can pull out scripture to utilize, as many have done, in proving almost any point we want to make. But using scripture out of context to mislead people is a dangerous venture. That occurs way too often in this world. (The most hideous misuse of God's Word is in the political arena, but that is a sermon for another day!) We do believe that the Word of God teaches that He wants to give good things to His children. In Matthew 7:7-11, Jesus said:

> *Ask, and it shall be given you; seek, and you shall find; knock, and it shall be opened unto you: For every one that asks, receives; and he that seeks, finds; and to him that knocks it shall be opened. Or what man is there of you, whom if his son ask bread, will he give him a stone? Or if he ask a fish, will he give him a serpent? If you then, being evil, know how to give good gifts to your children, how much more shall your Father which is in heaven give good things to them that ask him?*

Most folks would read this and sum it up by saying that God wants to bless His people. That is true, but there is a prerequisite to His blessing: the three words *ask, seek,* and *knock.*

> ASK – *requesting from God* (**communication**)
> SEEK – *to strive humbly and sincerely to follow and obey God* (**relationship**)
> KNOCK – *rapping to gain entrance* (**expectation**)

This is what is required of us – to be in a living, ongoing relationship with Him, knowing He will answer when we ask! When you know the King that way, He will not turn away and you know He will not - because *you know Him*!

And the three words that describe how God prospers us is *give good things* - translation: *bestow best quality.* He wants to do it! Jesus said He won't fail to

> *What we ask for must be good in God's eyes – not our own!*

give good things to His children, but the good that He gives us - the best quality He bestows - is what *He* measures, values, and deems best for us! If we assume that "ask and you will receive" means "ask for anything you want and I'll give it to you," then we have turned the Lord into a genie in a lamp who serves our every whim. This is the major problem with much of the "prosperity" message.

What we ask for must be good in God's eyes – not our own. God will give, but He only gives GOOD. If it is not for our good - no way! Whether or not He CAN do it is not in question. If you asked God for a jet (and it was His desire for you to have it), He would make a way. We couldn't do that for our kids, but He can give ANYTHING to His! Aren't you glad you're a child of the King of all Kings?! The point we are making is that yes, God wants to financially prosper us, but in *His* way and for *His* purpose. That means when He does prosper us, our response should be to lay up treasure in heaven, using what He gives us to further His Kingdom. If He blesses us, shouldn't we bless others?

Christians should be the most giving people on the face of the earth. We proclaim Christ is our eternal estate but focus way too much on the here and now. The only real, true, everlasting reward we will have is not in anything tangible here on earth, but in what we allow to go through us from God Almighty to spread the gospel of Christ and help others, being His hands. This is our test: Do we seek a present reward or an eternal estate? Jesus doesn't want to deprive us of treasure, but He wants us to choose to allow the direction of it - how it is used - to come from His Spirit. He is our provider and will give us what we need, and if we follow His lead, we may also be a partaker of expanding His Kingdom through our giving.

It is very tempting, especially when you're coming out of a lull in finances, to NOT lay up treasures. But don't wait until you have more to give, to respond to God in giving. There is a difference between a savings account and treasures - the difference is in Who and what you trust!

Earthly treasures are easy enough to discern - gold, silver, jewels and gems, real estate, money – these may secure our earthly future, but they will do nothing to secure our eternal future unless we use them, allowing God's will to be done with them, for the furthering of HIS Kingdom. Then earthly treasures become treasures in heaven! We are to be wise with money as well as all resources God has given us. We should work hard and take care of our families but do not forget that we, in Christ's Kingdom, are ALL family. We ARE our brother's and sister's keeper.

In 1973, David Wilkerson told of a prophetic vision from God about end-times. What was striking then, and is more so now, is what he said about Christians in these last days. He said Christians would "sit around singing and rejoicing – *but only with each other*, talk in tongues – *but still live like the devil*, and

have, as their greatest temptation, *financial success.*"
God help us!

Let your heart be open to how God wants you to offer yourself: your time, your abilities, your possesions, your knowledge, your information – your ALL.

May we let our bottom line not be what God will bestow upon us, but rather live a balanced life of giving and receiving in every area of our lives, like the ebb and flow of His mighty creation. Were the tide that comes in not allowed to return, imagine the catastrophe to humanity! We beseech you to "go with *God's* flow." Allow His blessings to refresh your thirsty soul, and then release to complete what He sends it to.

Those who are generous express the Savior's love.

By this we know the love of God, because he laid down his life for us: and we ought to lay down our lives for the brethren. But whoso has this world's good, and sees his brother have need, and shuts up his heart of compassion from him, how dwells the love of God in him? Let us not love in word, neither in tongue; but in deed and in truth. 1 John 3:16-18

Part Two

The Biblical Truth of Giving

~ 3 ~

Is Tithing Biblical
for Today?

Lord, have mercy! Why do we want to dispute whether or not the tithe is for us today? This is such a useless, anti-God argument. Yes, it is anti-God and anti-Christ. As stated earlier, giving that is initiated apart from God's Spirit has no weight. It has no eternal value. The only benefit is the here and now. The very nature of Jesus is to give His all that we may live. His ALL! Everything! Even, and most importantly, His life! If He gave His life willingly for you and me, why wouldn't we freely give just a small portion of our money for the benefit of His Kingdom? Why wouldn't we, who are called and chosen, being included in His kingdom, want to participate in the spreading of the Gospel, feeding the poor, and maintaining His house and those who carry and manage His earthly affairs? Jesus Himself warned us in Matthew 16:26:

> *What does a man profit, if he shall gain the whole world, and lose his own soul? Or what shall a man give in exchange for his soul?*

Listen, if we are not desiring to see others receive Christ so desperately that we will give of ourselves to see it done (including our time, our abilities, AND our money!), then we are living a life that is against the very nature of Christ Jesus (anti-Christ!).

We recall a conversation that occurred some years ago between a young man and an older minister. The young man was giving all the biblical reasons why drinking alcohol was okay because it was done in the Bible and Jesus did it. He was very proud of his research as he boasted his discovery. The Spirit of God spoke through the older woman and she said, "You know, I find that when people work so hard to prove that Jesus drank alcohol, they are trying to justify what they already do but feel convicted of." The countenance of the young man changed and his once-free tongue was bound as he hung his head in acknowledgement.

This is the human nature that we, who are in Christ, must die to. As long as we look to scripture to justify our actions or inactions, we're missing the mark. Scripture reveals to us the nature of God and Jesus. It is the divine internal nature we want to take on, not just the outward actions. "I can drink because Jesus did," only works if it is followed by, "I can die because Jesus died."

Just as this young man was trying to justify what he desired rather than what God desired, not tithing is often researched and proclaimed with the same heart: "Tithing is Old Testament!" We hear that all the time and it is always someone's attempt to justify why they don't do it. Nonetheless, we will explore how tithing came about in the Old Testament.

The first mention of 'tithe' in the Bible is from Genesis 12. The Hebrew word, *ma'aseŕ*, means "ten" or "tenth." When Abram (not yet renamed Abraham by God) heard that his nephew, Lot, had been taken, along with all Lot had, Abram took his men (318) and went after them. Not only did he conquer Lot's enemy and rescue him and what was his, but he gained everything the enemy had too! The Bible records that Melchizedek, the King of Salem, was also a priest of the Most High God. Abram *gave him tithes of all* he had gained.

The next mention is also in Genesis. Jacob was the son of Isaac, who was the son of Abraham. Jacob was the second son, Esau being the first, but through cunning trickery, ended up with the birthright of the firstborn. God revealed to him what that entailed in a dream. When Jacob awoke from the dream of promise, he set up an altar and made a promise himself - to God:

> *This stone, which I have set for a pillar, shall be God's house: and of all that you shall give me I will surely give the tenth to you.* **Genesis 28:22**

This was an ongoing promise, not a one-time offering. Jacob promised a tenth of ALL God would give him. Not only was his promise to give, but it was a recognition that it all came from God! He saw God as his source!

From these two accounts we see that the heart of those who believed and trusted God were moved to give according to the heart of God. God said of Abraham in Genesis 26:5:

> *Abraham obeyed my voice, and kept my charge, my commandments, my statutes, and my laws.*

And remember, this is before the Mosaic Law in Leviticus where the Lord initiated the requirement of giving a tenth of all produce, flocks, and cattle to support the Levites, His appointed priestly lineage. There were costs to maintaining a temple, just as there are costs today to maintain a church. There were expenses to feed and clothe those who worked there, to host the special events, holy days and convocations, to take care of orphans and widows. In addition, everyone was to be generous with those in need - not just tithing, but being generous!

> *If there is a poor man among your brothers in any of the towns of the land that the LORD your God is giving you, do not be hardhearted or tightfisted toward your poor brother. Rather be openhanded and freely lend him whatever he needs.*
> **Deuteronomy 15:7-8 NIV**

The nature God desired to see in the Israelites was His own nature. God is a constantly, consistently loving and giving God. Tithing and giving is a vital part of who we are because it is a vital part of Who He is! He desires that of us and He desired that of the Israelites. In Malachi, God rebuked Israel for not hearing His heart.

> *Will a man rob God? Yet ye have robbed me. But ye say, Wherein have we robbed thee? In tithes and offerings. Ye are cursed with a curse: for ye have robbed me, even this whole nation. Bring ye all the tithes into the storehouse, that there may be meat in mine house, and prove me now herewith, saith the LORD of hosts, if I will not open you the windows of heaven, and pour you out a blessing, that there shall not be room enough to receive it.* **Malachi 3:8-10**

Every believer has a responsibility to support his or her local church financially. This is God's nature and heart. He has always desired to grow His nature in man, helping us to realize He is our Lord, Provider, and Creator, Who loves us unconditionally.

> Generosity is giving more than is necessary or expected.

He is our *higher* standard – higher than the world - by which we gauge our motivations.

Keeping this command of tithing does not tie us to the law (unless we do it ritually). Having a heart to give to God connects us to the GOD of the Old Testament Who, by the way, is the God of the New Testament too! So before you say, "Tithing is Old Testament law and we're freed from that," we would like to remind you that Jesus came to FULFILL the law, not to do away with it (HIS words, not ours. See Matthew 5:17).

And Jesus also said:

> *Woe unto you, scribes and Pharisees, hypocrites!* ***for ye pay tithe*** *of mint and anise and cummin, and* <u>*have omitted*</u> *the weightier matters of the law, judgment, mercy, and faith:* ***these ought ye to have done****, and not to leave the other undone.*
> **Matthew 23:23**

Jesus called out the scribes and Pharisees but He was also talking to a crowd of people, including His disciples. His message is for everyone and it's this: The God-focused man or woman will be God-motivated! Jesus is talking about the totality of His nature – the nature of God. God's nature is giving, loving, and being merciful toward people. It's about ALL that we do and the motivation behind what we do. Jesus called these guys out for being obedient to tithe but not treating their brother righteously. Note that He did not say, "Don't tithe, just have a God-focused heart," because you cannot have a God-focused heart and NOT give of your finances. You'll do everything you can to help the Kingdom, to support your local church, to feed the hungry, to spread the Gospel of Jesus Christ in order to see the lost saved!

We were instructed in the Old Testament (and it did not change in the New Testament) to bring the tithe to the temple in order to maintain the temple, the priests, and all that the priests oversaw. Levites were not allowed real estate holdings and accumulated possessions because theirs was a calling to maintain God's presence in this world for present and future generations. All of Israel, in fact, was designated as the official people to carry and maintain God's Word to the world. The local church is today's temple and our tithe takes care of the building, the staff, and all that is overseen locally in taking the LIVING WORD to people everywhere.

We should realize that when we tithe to our local church, we are partaking in carrying the Living Word to present and future generations!

Remember, to give the tithe was introduced as law in the Old Testament, but, as all law, it was given to teach men how they ought to live (having the nature of God). Just as Jesus described that, with His grace, not only do men have the ability not to commit adultery, but also to exist without even having lust in their heart; with His grace we can do more than to just tithe. The reality is that not just 10%, but EVERYTHING we have is God's anyway. The psalmist begins the 24th Psalm with:

> *The earth is the LORD's, and all its full-ness* (everything in it), *the world and those who dwell therein.*

He created it, He filled it – it's His! When He placed Adam in the garden, east of Eden, it was to *work it and to take care of it*. He created man, and man was given dominion in the garden. That meant that he was to be the *steward – the manager or overseer*. The ownership wasn't given to Adam, just the right to take care of it. It still belonged to God and it still does today!

God owns everything; we are simply managers or administrators acting on His behalf. As a child of the King, we express our love and obedience to Him, by responsibly (dependably and maturely) administering everything He has placed under our control. This isn't just about managing our finances; it's an all-encompassing position. We commit ourselves and possessions to God's service, recognizing that we do not have the right of *control* over our property or ourselves - none of it is ours anyway!

> *What? know ye not that your body is the temple of the Holy Ghost which is in you, which ye have of God, and ye are not your own? For ye are bought with a price: therefore glorify God in your body, and in your spirit, which are God's.* I Corinthians 6:19-20

Living under grace means that rather than the emphasis being on "not having the right to administer our own desires," we have the privilege of administering according to His desires so His will is accomplished. So when we look around and see what *we* have accumulated, we must be careful not to attribute it to our own works.

We should be cautioned not to be tempted to say, as God warned in **Deuteronomy 8:17:**

> *My power and the strength of my hands have produced this wealth for me.*

But maintain the truth in our heart that God stated in **Deuteronomy 8:18**:

> *Remember the LORD your God, for it is **he** who gives you the ability to produce wealth.*

God gives us abilities. God gives us talents. God gives us everything! He allows us to enjoy it, as Adam was given the garden to enjoy, but we are to enjoy it *while* we manage that which belongs to God under the influence and by the Spirit *of* God.

Though the main focus of this writing is about giving financially, it must be pointed out, once again, that His nature in us should influence how we are responsible for everything in our lives - resources, abilities, opportunities, information, authority, and relationships - *everything* that God has entrusted to our care! And one day, each one of us will be called to give an account for how we have managed what the Master has given us. We are not allowed to rule over it as *we* see fit. We are called to fulfill our role as manager (dominion) under the watchful eye of the Creator and do that in accord with the doctrines He has established. His doctrine, principles, and values ALWAYS line up with His character, nature, and heart.

Jesus taught us this by the Parable of the Talents in Matthew 25:14 – 23:

> *For the kingdom of heaven is like a man traveling to a far country, who called his own servants and delivered his goods to them. And to one he gave five talents, to another two, and to another one, to each according to his own ability; and immediately he went on a journey. Then he who had received the five talents went and traded with them, and made another five talents. And likewise he who had received two gained two more also. But he who had received one went and dug in the ground, and hid his lord's money.*
>
> *After a long time the lord of those servants came and settled accounts with them. So he who had received five talents came and brought five other talents, saying, "Lord, you delivered to me five talents; look, I have gained five more talents besides them." His Lord said to him, "Well done, good and faithful servant; you were faithful over a*

few things, I will make you ruler over many things. Enter into the joy of your lord."

He also who had received two talents came and said, "Lord, you delivered to me two talents; look, I have gained two more talents besides them." His lord said to him, "Well done, good and faithful servant; you have been faithful over a few things, I will make you ruler over many things. Enter into the joy of your lord."

Then he who had received the one talent came and said, "Lord, I knew you to be a hard man, reaping where you have not sown, and gathering where you have not scattered seed. And I was afraid, and went and hid your talent in the ground. Look there you have what is yours." But his lord answered and said to him, "You wicked and lazy servant, you knew that I reap where I have not sown, and gather where I have not scattered seed. So you ought to have deposited my money with bankers, and at my coming I would have received back my own with interest. Therefore take the talent from him, and give it to him who has ten talents."

Each one of us will be called to give an account of how we have administered everything we have been given. We will all give an account to the rightful owner *Who* has entrusted to us not just money and possessions, but also spouses, children, families, friends, acquaintances and opportunities! He has entrusted EVERYTHING in our lives to us, even our jobs and our Christian service!

> *Whatever you do, work at it with all your heart, as working for the Lord, not for men, since you know that you will receive an inheritance from the Lord as a reward. It is the Lord Christ you are serving.*
> **Colossians 3:23-24**

But we who trust Him and are faithful to do the Master's will with the Master's resources can expect His promise of reward – maybe not fully on this side of eternity, but surely on the other. And we all should long to hear what He exclaims in Matthew 25:21:

> *Well done, good and faithful servant! You have been faithful with a few things; I will put you in charge of many things. Come and share your master's happiness!*

Having been in ministry for a number of years, we find it interesting that people will talk more readily to you about the most tragic moments in their lives, their weakest areas of transgressions, and their deepest emotions, than they will talk to you about money and tithing. We have concluded that there are two reasons for this. Sometimes it's because they are obedient to give God what is His and don't want to boast. But mostly, and this is sad, it's because people don't give according to God's will. They know they should but are not doing so. The sacrifice of Christ on the cross did not do away with God wanting us to live righteous lives with generous hearts. But rather, by the gift of the Holy Spirit, He said we can be so motivated by His goodness that tithing is just a starting point! The more you release

The cross did not do away with God's desire for us to live & give righteously.

your heart and desires to His, the more you'll respond and give righteously. So to those nay-sayers who hold that the tithe is Old Testament and not for us today, we say, you're right! Because of Jesus' sacrifice and the gift of the Holy Spirit, our hearts have the ability to expand with His righteousness so that we are not bound and "conformed" to give *only* the first tenth, but we are loosed to be "transformed" into His image, making our hearts and hands open to give all that we have!

Those who are generous are refreshed!

One person gives freely, yet gains even more; another withholds unduly, but comes to poverty. A generous person will prosper; whoever refreshes others will be refreshed. Proverbs 11:24-25

~ 4 ~

And Offerings Too?

Yep, offerings too. The Holy Spirit, as we stated in the previous chapter, will prompt us to give aside from tithing and firstfruits when and where there are needs. In the Old Testament there were voluntary offerings as well as mandatory offerings. We won't go too far in depth on this topic, but we will look at offerings with the intent of further revealing the nature of God and the relevance for offerings today. We want to reiterate, however, that because of Christ, there is no structure for voluntary and mandatory giving. His heart freely gives so our hearts should freely give. We don't *have to* give anything, but we *get to* give everything!

The offerings and sacrifices of the Old Testament have three things which make them unique: Purpose, Parcel, & Portion. The purpose is the *why*. The parcel is the *what*. And the portion is the *who*.

The *purpose* of the mandatory offerings and sacrifices was to atone for known sin and unintentional sin and to cleanse from defilement and physical disorders. That's why it was mandatory – it was necessary for man's survival. Compare that to voluntary offerings which were an expression of worship to God. We know that Jesus took care of mandatory offerings and sacrifices once and for all. No longer is it required for us to offer the lives of animals to redeem our own. But voluntary offerings as a way of worshiping God has not only NOT ceased, but because of the transforming power of the Holy Spirit in our lives, it should have INCREASED! We don't mean to be pessimistic by saying this, but it is doubtful that the church today worships God in offerings more than those in ancient Israel did. Just saying.

The *parcel* is what was offered or sacrificed. Specific items were offered for specific purposes. From fine flour to unblemished lambs, each element offered was valuable to the giver. The degree of value it held determined what was offered in many cases. The poor, for example, may only have been required to give fine flour for the sin offering, while those who had more may have given a she-goat. Both were considered the same value of offering based on the giver's financial standing (what they had). This is what Jesus was pointing out when the widow offered her mite. The rich gave from their abundance, but from her lack, the widow gave all she had. That was much, much more than a tithe - she gave all!

That is the heart of God right there! That is the heart He wants to see in us - a desire to give more than the tithe and more than what is 'required.' But because our carnal minds struggle with the concept of offering and giving above what is required, we may just merely give enough to get by with no complete commitment. That struggle will not be won until we are fully surrendered to the Holy Spirit. May we constantly be reminded that everything belongs to God and if we presume to own it apart from Him, we do not know or exhibit His nature. Abundant love deserves abundant adoration. It deserves our all.

The *portion* determined who benefitted from the *parcel*. You would think that since the offerings and sacrifices were made to God, He alone would benefit, wouldn't you? Nope. That's not God's nature. With mandatory offerings there was God's portion and the priest's portion. With voluntary offerings there was God's

> God's nature is for everyone to have provision.

portion, the Priest's portion, and with some, the participant's portion. The priests and Levites worked on behalf of God, maintaining the temple and temple matters. And God made provisions for them. In everything they did and were responsible for, provision was made. Although we don't have the same temple structure today, we do have men and women of God who work on behalf of God, overseeing local churches and caring for flocks. We give tithes to God through the local church to care for them. But if we have a heart like God, we will want to make offerings, voluntarily, to show our thanksgiving to God by providing for His workers. What a giving God we have! For peace offerings in the Old Testament, *everyone* who participated, benefited. Not only was this a recognition of God's provision, it *was* God providing! God is our provider!

When your heart is set on that, it will proclaim that not only consistently, but persistently. You can't stop it! You see how, with every offering made to God, He fits it into a blessing for someone else. His heart is operating through us. His nature begins to be our nature. The Holy Spirit will lead us to needs and we will joyfully give what is already His to be used for His desired purpose.

Being generous is not burdensome.

For if there be first a willing mind, it is accepted according to that a man has, and not according to that he has not. For I mean not that other men be eased, and you burdened: But by an equality, that now at this time your abundance may be a supply for their want, that their abundance also may be a supply for your want: that there may be equality: As it is written, He that had gathered much had nothing over; and he that had gathered little had no lack.
2 Corinthians 8:12-15

~ 5 ~
# Firstfruits: Misunderstood Giving

If you have not studied scripture specifically concerning *firstfruits*, you may think that firstfruits and tithes are the same. They are not. *Firstfruits* is related to a yearly harvest, and is given before we enter the blessing of the coming year. Tithes has to do with ongoing income. Firstfruits is a thanksgiving for where God has brought us *from* (out of our own Egypt), and for how He *will be* our continual provision. It isn't the first tenth of our earnings; it isn't even a tenth. No portion measurement is given. It's just the first thing we receive. (Abraham was asked to give his firstborn, not 10 percent of his children.)

In order to fully understand firstfruits offering, we must look at the Feast of Firstfruits. The feasts began each spring with Passover. In the table below, note that each 'day' is a 24-hour period. We have tracked the Old Testament feasts with the New Testament fulfillments.

Old Testament								
Day 1	Day 2	Day 3	Day 4	Day 5	Day 6	Day 7	Day 8	50 Days after Passover
Passover								
	Unleavened Bread							
		Firstfruits						
								Moses/LAW
New Testament								
Crucifixion		Resurrection						Holy Spirit

Passover was celebrated because God saved the Hebrews from the Egyptians. He told them to take a lamb . . .

> *Take some of the blood. Put it on the sides and tops of the doorframes of the houses where you eat the lambs . . . That same night I will pass through Egypt. I will strike down all those born first among the*

*people and animals. And I will judge all the gods of Egypt. I am the LORD. The blood on your houses will be a sign for you. **When I see the blood, I will pass over you.** No deadly plague will touch you when I strike Egypt.* **Exodus 12**

When He sees the blood, HE WILL PASS OVER YOU! The blood shed by the Passover Lamb saved their firstborn from death. What a prophetic picture of Christ on the cross! Jesus, our Passover Lamb, shed His blood, and redeemed us. We no longer have to slay lambs; we have been forever saved from the enemy of our soul, the enemy of Christ. That's our eternal cause for celebration, isn't it?

Passover lasted 24 hours. When Passover ended (the next day), the feast of *Unleaven Bread* began and lasted for seven days. The first Passover was in Egypt and because of the death of Pharaoh's firstborn son, he urgently told Moses to take all Israelites out of Egypt (lest they ALL die). God told the people to leave so quickly that they shouldn't even allow their bread to rise. When He instituted the feast, He said, *"for you came out of the land of Egypt in haste."*

On the second day of the feast of Unleavened Bread began the feast of *Firstfruits*. This 'feast within a feast' ended the next day (or the third day after Passover began). We know that centuries later this was the day Jesus rose from the grave!

> *And the Lord spoke to Moses, saying, Speak to the children of Israel, and say to them, When you come into the land which I give to you, and shall reap the harvest thereof, then you shall bring a sheaf of the* **firstfruits** *of your harvest unto the priest: And he shall wave the sheaf before the Lord, to be accepted for you: on the morrow after the sabbath the priest shall wave it. And ye shall offer that day when ye wave the sheaf a he lamb without blemish of the first year for a burnt offering unto the Lord.* **Leviticus 23:9-12**

We want to call attention to the Hebrew word for *firstfruits*. It is the word *re'šiyt*. What is remarkable is that this is also the first word in the whole Bible. It means, "in the beginning." The Greek equivalent (adopted by Old English) is actually "Genesis." It's the first, the chief, the best, the *firstfruits*.

When firstfruits was celebrated:

- It marked **the beginning** of the harvest season.
- The **first** crops harvested were brought as the offering.
- They were acknowledging that it was GOD who gave the harvest they were about to gather.

Until this feast had been completed, they could not partake of, use, or harvest any of their grain. As stated earlier, there was no measurement given for the portion to give to God, just whatever came first. The firstfruits was a recognition of, and a thanksgiving for, God's provision. It was a declaration of trusting God for giving His children the opportunity to be blessed before they even received the blessing! That's trust! And that's why many Christians today celebrate firstfruits in the beginning of the year – to thank God for what He is going to do, even before He does it, and to trust Him to be our provision and blessing for the coming year.

> *Giving to God before we receive anything reveals our trust that He will provide everything!*

Just because this was instituted in the Old Testament does not mean it is not for us today. The Old Testament, as you may know, was a revelation by type and shadow of the New Testament. And remember, Jesus came to *fulfill* the law. Consider the following scripture from I Corinthians 15:20-23:

> *But now is Christ risen from the dead, and become the **firstfruits** of them that slept. For since by man came death, by man came also the resurrection of the dead. For as in Adam all die, even so in Christ shall all be made alive. But every man in his own order: Christ the **firstfruits**; or as in Adam all die, even so in Christ shall all be made alive.*

Jesus became our Passover Lamb. He lived the perfect, unleavened, sinless life, eating the *bread of affliction* upon the cross so that we might be saved. He IS the firstfruits of the resurrection. Now remember, for there to be a harvest, there must have been a sowing. C.H. Spurgeon stated, *"If the resurrection of Christ is the firstfruits, then the resurrection of the elect must be looked upon as a harvest, and death would, therefore, be symbolized by a sowing."*

He was the firstfruits of those who had already died, for when He was crucified, the Old Testament saints who had died from Adam to that day were resurrected after Christ was resurrected.

And, behold, the veil of the temple was rent in twain from the top to the bottom; and the earth did quake, and the rocks rent; And the graves were opened; and many bodies of the saints which slept arose, And came out of the graves after his resurrection, and went into the holy city, and appeared unto many.
Matthew 27:51-53

Without Christ, the Firstfruit of the resurrected (our Genesis, the beginning, the chief, the best), there would not -COULD not - be a harvest of saints. But because of Him, there isn't only a harvest, but it is one without number! Because Jesus gave His very life as a sacrifice, an offering of the "first" to be harvested, we know we can trust God in that what follows will be an increase that cannot be measured. The same is true when we give God our firstfruits. Whatever it is, if it's first, what follows will be an increase that we could not possibly predict. When we offer firstfruits to God we are saying, *before anything else is received,*

- that we thank Him for delivering us from our own Egypt (life of bondage),
- that because of Jesus, our sins (our leaven) are washed away,
- that because He has given to us first (salvation, freedom), we trust Him - and because we do - we're going to give HIM our

firstfruits at the beginning of our harvest or new year.

Remember that firstfruits is not the tithe or ten percent of our income. That, technically, is not an offering because it belongs to the Lord anyway. When we bring our tithe to the Lord we really have not given Him anything yet. We are simply giving Him what is already His. Even so, He blesses us for our obedience in bringing our tithe into the "storehouse" as He said in Malachi. But firstfruits is different. The tithe *opens the windows of heaven*, but the firstfruits offering brings *more than enough* for you so you can give to others. That's because when we trust God enough to give firstfruits, He knows He can trust us enough to bless others, and He will give us more than enough for our needs.

We are blessed when we tithe according to what we have received. With firstfruits, since we give before we even get, the blessing we receive from it has no bounds - God determines the blessing according to the fruit we give FIRST! Romans 11:16 likens firstfruits to our new life in Christ - *For if the firstfruit be holy* (what we give to God FIRST), *the lump* (what comes after) *is also holy: and if the root be holy* (Jesus), *so are the branches* (believers - you and me). Whatever is connected to the root is holy because the root is holy. Whatever is connected to the firstfruits is holy because we have given the firstfruit to GOD and HE is Holy. Thus the remainder of what we have is Holy (sacred, set apart, consecrated). Now, that is blessed!

That's why God told Israel not to touch anything in Jericho. Jericho was the firstfruits (not tithe) of the Promised Land. It belonged to God and Joshua warned his men:

> *The city shall be **accursed** (Hebrew word cherem), even it, and all that are therein, to the Lord: only Rahab the harlot shall live, she and all that are with her in the house, because she hid the messengers that we sent. And ye, in any wise keep yourselves from the **accursed** thing, lest ye make yourselves accursed, when ye take of the **accursed** thing, and make the camp of Israel a **curse**, and trouble it.*
> Joshua 6:17-18

Whenever you see the words accursed or curse, it is the Hebrew word cḥerem (herem). It is a noun that refers to *things devoted to destruction*. The basic meaning is *the identity of things which were to be set aside to destroy*. The entire city of Jericho (except Rahab and her family) was set aside for destruction. By doing so in obedience, it would ensure that the remainder of the Promised Land would be holy because the first portion was dedicated to God. This also kept the leaven out of the whole.

Idols of the conquered pagans were not allowed into the dwelling places of the Israelites for this reason. [This same word, cherem is, interestingly, the last word in the text of the Prophets – the last word in our Old Testament (Malachi 4:6), a warning for those who don't fear the name of the Lord.]

For years it was taught (and we believed) that the city of Jericho was the tithe. And further, we associated the cherem with the tithe only. But from studying Scripture it is clear that Jericho was not the tithe, but the firstfruit. They didn't come to the end of the land and say, "Here God, here's our tithe." They had not even fully seen all there was to God's promise yet, but they gave the first portion based on His promise of all the land. Jericho was devoted – set aside for God.

> No devoted thing, that a man shall devote unto the Lord of all that he has, both of man and beast, and of the field of his possession, shall be sold or redeemed: every devoted thing is most holy to the Lord. None devoted, which shall be devoted of men, shall be redeemed; but shall surely be put to death. And all the tithe of the land, whether of the seed of the land, or of the fruit of the tree, is the Lord's: it is holy unto the Lord.
> Leviticus 27:28-30

Because all things of this earth (all possessions, all lands, all monies, all people) are connected to this world, they depend on this (fallen) world to thrive. But by devoting them for destruction, God promises that they (and we) no longer depend on a dying world to survive and thrive, but on a Holy God. For the Israelites, the 'thing' devoted was Jericho, the firstfruits, that, when consecrated, made the Promised Land holy. Jericho was separated from the fallen earth, and made Holy by God, so that all of the land would be consecrated to Him. Don't we want that in our lives?

The Israelites really had no idea of what the Promised Land held. Surely, if they would have chosen their own blessing for what the Promised Land held, it would not have been as vast as it was. We, too, have no idea of the vast blessing God wants to give us. Achan decided to choose his own blessing, so he kept a portion of what was to be devoted to God. Think about it. Do you really want to keep what is God's? Do you really NOT want what you have to be holy? God was saying to the Israelites, and He's saying to us today, give me your tithes, give me your firstfruits, and let Me decide what your portion will be. God's portion for us is far greater than we can even imagine and is manifest in far more ways than mere money.

There was something that was always a little un-soothing to us about the 'devoted to destruction' aspect to things that are devoted to God. How could destruction have anything to do with God? Then He gave us this revelation: It isn't being given to God and then destroyed; it's being released from us and being destroyed. The emphasis is not on what is given to God but what is *released* from the giver! That 'thing' that is devoted for destruction is the world's hold on our lives. As long as we hold onto it, we are tethered to the world. When the world is destroyed, so will we be. But when we release that to God, when we devote ourselves to Him, we are untethering ourselves from the flesh, from this world, and allowing God to purify (destroy) the world in our lives.

In the Old Testament, God established a physical order (feasts, ordinances, laws, etc.) and put them in physical motion. We know that represented the coming Christ and renewal of the spiritual order; not that we discontinue following His doctrine, but that through Christ, we are able to not just 'do' these things according to His law, but we are able to fulfill these things according to the Spirit. It is the Spirit that is our spark of inspiration and our beginning point. So rather than being motivated by "order of the law," we are motivated by the "move of the Spirit."

Since we began this study on firstfruits, we actually have a better understanding of the tithe. The tithe is ten percent of the lump that is received – not just our regular income, but gain. If we are given a financial gift from someone, we always make sure that we give God the first tenth of that too! Whenever we have an increase, we tithe to God before anything else. So if we receive a paycheck and the amount is $1,000, before we do anything else, we make sure at least $100 is given to our local church as our tithe.

> *Giving is not a requirement of God's law, it's a motivation of His Spirit.*

But firstfruits, as stated, is not regular income. Firstfruits is the first that's received. In the Old Testament, it was the first harvest of each year and **until it was given to the Lord, you could not touch any of the rest of your harvest**. No amount was given, just whatever was ripe and ready on that day. But here's the thing, everything they would receive in that harvest period was blessed because the first portion had been set aside for the Lord and blessed. Since we don't plant a harvest of grain or have crops to give as firstfruits but rather receive money as gain, we conclude that the first money that is gained each year is our firstfruits. We're giving all of the first – not a tenth of the lump. By doing so, we release God's blessing all year long. By giving Him firstfruits you'll ensure that, for the rest of the year, you'll have opportunity after opportunity to bless Him! Before it's even made, our gain is blessed! Doesn't that make you want to shout!

If not, chances are you either don't trust God or you think all this giving stuff is strictly Old Testament. Let's look at the latter first. If you don't think tithing firstfruits apply to us today, consider the words of Jesus:

> *Think not that I am come to destroy the law, or the prophets: I am not come to destroy, but to fulfill. For verily I say unto you, Till heaven and earth pass, one jot or one tittle shall in no wise pass from the law, till all be fulfilled. Whosoever therefore shall break one of these least commandments, and shall teach men so, he shall be called the least in the kingdom of heaven: but whosoever shall do and teach them, the same shall be called great in the kingdom of heaven.* Matthew 5:17-19

Woe unto you, scribes and Pharisees, hypocrites! for ye pay tithe of mint and anise and cummin, and have omitted the weightier matters of the law, judgment, mercy, and faith: these ought ye to have done, and not to leave the other undone.
Matthew 23:23

Wouldn't you rather give tithes and firstfruits on this side of heaven than not to do so and arrive there only to find out you were wrong? Only God can judge your heart, but it makes one wonder if you really trust God when you don't trust His Word? Giving, along with all that we do and all that we are, is about WHO we trust, isn't it? And God is lovingly, wonderfully anticipating, as His eyes roam to and fro, who will trust Him.

The eyes of the Lord run to and fro throughout the whole earth, to show himself strong in the behalf of them whose heart is perfect toward him. 2 Chronicles 16:9

God is looking for people who will rely on Him. Abraham relied on God fully and became fully what God desired. The same can be true for us today. God knows what He wants you to be and to do as well.

And He's giving you opportunities to give great things to Him so He can give great things to you. Do you really trust God? Do you really walk in covenant with Him? If you cannot trust Him with your material wealth, how can you say you trust Him with your soul? If, at your core, your trust is in the Lord, He will show Himself strong on your behalf.

God wants our trust to be in Him. He wants us to treasure, above all else, that eternal covenant with Him. That causes us to place, at our core, in our hearts, the most value in "things above." That is something that cannot be taken away or destroyed. If your heart trusts God and His love flows through you, you will cheerfully, happily, contentedly want to give.

> *But this I say, He which sows sparingly shall reap also sparingly; and he which sows bountifully shall reap also bountifully. Every man according as he purposes in his heart, so let him give; not grudgingly, or of necessity: for God loves a cheerful giver.* 2 Corinthians 9:7

Paul wasn't talking about the tithe. He was talking about giving from a heart that desires to give because it's full of God!

*Honor the Lord with thy substance, and
with the firstfruits of all thine increase: So
shall thy barns be filled with plenty, and
thy presses shall burst out with new wine.*
Proverb 3:9

In many ways, we think firstfruits giving is more
important than tithing because it sets the pace for
ALL giving. In the Old Testament, before we even
see the tithe introduced, firstfruits was established.
The whole premise of firstfruits is that the first
belongs to God. Why? Because that reveals He is
(or should be) every "first" in our lives. He is the
creator – the reason for everything! When the law
was given, the first commandment was, "I shall be
first."

- In the garden, the tree of the knowledge of
  good and evil was not to be touched – it
  belonged to God. This was not the first tenth,
  it was the firstfruit of the garden.
- When Cain worked the fields and Abel
  raised sheep, their "firsts" were to be given
  to God – not the first tenth, the firstfruit.
- When they were led out of Egypt, God
  commanded, "Sanctify unto me all the
  firstborn, whatsoever opens the womb
  among the children of Israel, both of man

and of beast: it is mine." This was not the first tenth, it was the firstfruit.

- As stated earlier, the first city of the Promised Land, "Jericho," was God's. It was not the first tenth, it was the firstfruit.

And when God created animals AND man, the first words He spoke were, "Be fruitful," and they were followed by, "multiply." The natural order He set in place was to be fruitful, the outcome of which is multiplication. We know that the natural order is a replica of the spiritual order. It is by spirit that God is manifest in our lives – in every part of our lives. When we are born again, we become part of His spiritual Kingdom where we are also to be fruitful and multiply. When we make God *first* in our lives, and as we yield ourselves to Him, we produce *Fruit of the Spirit*. Being fruitful means that love, joy, peace, longsuffering, gentleness, goodness, faith, meekness, and temperance begin to grow by His Spirit in us. And as it is multiplied, it benefits those around us. That's how the gospel is spread. When Jesus gave the great commission, *"Therefore go and make disciples of all nations, baptizing them in the name of the Father and of the Son and of the Holy Spirit, and teaching them to obey everything I have commanded you,"* He knew it could be accomplished because of the great commandment to put God first. Putting God first means that we ARE fruitful, and making disciples is how we multiply.

So, what are your firstfruits to God? It could be your first pay check, or the first hour's or day's wages. Only God should reveal it to you. Ask Him. He will quicken an answer to you. And when you do give firstfruits, not only will you receive abundance, you will receive enough to bless others. You can't out-give God. He owns it all. The more you give, the more He blesses. He wants to bless you more than He ever has before. He does! He is a loving Father. He wants us to trust Him so He can bless us. Do you trust Him? Firstfruits shows God you are not in love with money; you are in love with Him! Thus, He can trust you with money and with giving you more money. Firstfruits is an expression of your love for Him and His Word.

> *Firstfruits reveals to God that we trust Him and we're in love with Him!*

If you are reading this and it's not the first of the year, or maybe you aren't even a tither, don't put it off any longer. You can begin tithing right away. And don't wait until you feel like you've seen your promised land to give firstfruits. Give the first things to God based on His promise. This can be your new beginning. You don't have to do it. God doesn't force us to love Him and trust Him. But wouldn't a person who trusts God be happy to do it? Maybe you're thinking, "I haven't been faithful to even tithe, much less give firstfruits." But the time to begin is when your eyes are opened. Are your eyes open? Has the Lord quickened His Word to you? If so, then the time to begin is now!

~ 6 ~
To Sum it Up

If you have read the entirety of this book, our hope is that you don't see giving as a tithe or an offering, but have the revelation, as we have, that everything we receive and allow to go through us is our opportunity to reveal to God that He is first in our heart. That's what He's really after. That is how He desires for each of us to be transformed. While yes, we need to be educated with His Word, the greater, deeper application is that by His Spirit, God's heart and nature is imparted to us. When you maintain a "God First" attitude in your heart, everything you are, everything you do, everything you become, will be affected by His nature. Being generous with your time, abilities, possessions, and money will become your natural landscape. It might sound restricting to the less mature, but, in fact, it is most liberating to the soul and spirit!

Firstfruits in your life isn't just about giving money, it's more about giving yourself. Once you develop a *God-first* heart, giving will be only one part of a life fully devoted to Him.

> *But whoso keeps his word, in him truly is the love of God perfected: hereby know we that we are in him. He that says he abides in him ought himself also so to walk, even as he walked.* I John 2:5-6

Firstfruits is about beginning each *day* speaking with God, recognizing His wonder and glory.

> *From the rising of the sun unto the going down of the same the Lord's name is to be praised.* Psalms 113:3

Firstfruits is beginning each *week* thanking God for what He has done and also for what He is going to do.

> *I will praise thee, O Lord, with my whole heart; I will show forth all thy marvelous works. I will be glad and rejoice in thee: I will sing praise to thy name, O thou most High.* Psalm 9:1-2

Firstfruits is beginning each *month* acknowledging that He is our provision; that He goes before us and prepares our path, and is never surprised by what comes our way.

> *It is the Lord who goes before you; he will be with you, he will not fail you, neither forsake you: fear not, neither be dismayed.* Deuteronomy 31:8

Just as the original firstfruits of the Old Testament was not a specific amount (just whatever came first), having a God-first heart is about what comes first – in your thoughts, your words, your actions, even your giving! A God-first heart is absorbed in how it may bring honor and glory to God - *first*.

> *Seek ye first the kingdom of God, and his righteousness; and all these things shall be added unto you.* Matthew 6:32

FIRSTFRUITS
TESTIMONIES

Michael & Rose

During the first week in January of 2017, we heard our first message on firstfruits. We learned that firstfruits is different from tithing because you are stepping out on faith, committing your first earnings of the year to God before you've even received it. In the Breezewood pamphlet, there was a detailed description of how to calculate your firstfruits depending on which way God led you. At lunch after church, we discussed this idea of giving that was new to us. We had already decided we would be ALL IN for God in 2017, so the decision to pay our first-time firstfruits was a no-brainer. We were already entrusting God with several decisions for the year, such as Rose's desire to quit her job and become a stay-at-home mom. When we calculated our first week's salary it was around $1850. That blew us away, because we barely had that much money to our name! Not wanting to leave our family of four in a risky place, and also not wanting to shortchange God, we prayed. After praying about the amount, we felt God urging us that He promised to provide. His grace is more than enough.

We wrote the check, turned it in to the church, and never looked back. In the coming weeks, Rose's desire to become a stay-at-home mom started to become a reality. Our concern for the cost of private health insurance on a family of four with an insulin-dependent diabetic became the only thing holding her back from turning in her notice at work.

We called our insurance agent to get a quote, already assuming it was a call wasted. To our surprise she called back quickly with amazing news! Our family qualified for $1776 in discounts - MONTHLY. This meant our out-of-pocket expense would be $43 per month for health insurance for our family of four!! This blew us away!! We wrote God one check for around $1850 and He had already blessed us with almost that same amount MONTHLY for the whole year of 2017. Tears of joy just consumed us!

The rest of the year went the same way. We never missed Rose's $60k salary after she became a stay-at-home mom. The improvements in our kids were off the charts. Michael's plumbing business became so busy he almost couldn't keep up. We saw healings in our bodies, strength in our relationships, growth in our finances to the point we were able to give more than ever before, and the list goes on and on. We also received news of our newest baby in the last month of 2017 with a direct message from God on a smooth delivery with no complications (which was a fear of ours since Rose had an eye stroke during her first pregnancy delivery).

God was so true to His promise of being more than enough for us! He gave us more than we could have ever imagined! Needless to say the firstfruits check for 2018 was written before we could finish out 2017. You can never out give God.

Diane

I had read the word "firstfruits" in the Bible many times, never paying attention to it. I am a tither and have several stories of God moving in some specific times of tithing in my life. That, in itself, is amazing. I became a 20% tither, but when my husband retired, I was unable to continue and was particularly distraught about that. Then God whispered, "You are a 20% tither - it is for your husband." I was able to breathe and walk forward after that.

I had not even been attending the church very long when I heard the Pastor's sermon on firstfruits in January 2017. I questioned the validity: "Perhaps it's just a church wanting money." This church was certainly different than any denomination I had ever previously been involved with in my life, and I had preconceived ideas in my mind. But the Pastor provided Scripture references in his sermon, and when I studied firstfruits and Scripture on my own, my mind was opened by God to see clearly.

I gave firstfruits.

Through many years prior, I had carried an amends I thought I needed to make. God had told me in December 2016, I would take care of it this year (2017). The potential business mistake I thought I had made had occurred many years earlier and was during a period of time following my son's death when sometimes my mind *did not clearly remember things. But I felt strongly all these years that I needed to make this amends. I went about doing it and was provided a copy of the contract. When I reviewed the contract, it was clear I had not erred. God had waited until this time to clear this thing that had followed me all these years, and He had chosen to wait until after I gave the firstfruits. I was prepared to make this amends, which was very large ($75,000). This was God's moving and God's money. Since I had already set aside this sum of money, it was given to fund a church in a foreign country and to help fund the future building of my new church!*

Casi & Stuart

Throughout our entire married life we have always tried to honor God in our finances – faithful to tithe, make offerings, and give firstfruits. And God has been faithful to complete His promises for our lives. He has abundantly provided for us. Each year we give our first income to the Lord through our local church and truly believe that the blessings of God in our life are a result of our commitment to give. We have experienced surprise promotions, better work environments, bonuses, and the favor of God in our careers and in our lives. We do not give because of what God does for us. But rather, we give out of a joyful and thankful heart – grateful that we have the opportunity to give! We have learned that He isn't looking at the size of the gift, but the size of our heart when we give to Him. God has shown us that as we give cheerfully, obediently, and wholeheartedly, He opens the windows of heaven and pours blessings into our marriage and home.

> *In everything you do, put God first, and he will direct you and crown your efforts with success.*
> Proverbs 3:6 (TLB)

Made in the USA
Columbia, SC
10 November 2018